EVOLVE

WORKBOOK

Samuela Eckstut

4B

CAMBRIDGE
UNIVERSITY PRESS

CAMBRIDGE
UNIVERSITY PRESS & ASSESSMENT

Shaftesbury Road, Cambridge CB2 8EA, United Kingdom

One Liberty Plaza, 20th Floor, New York, NY 10006, USA

477 Williamstown Road, Port Melbourne, VIC 3207, Australia

314–321, 3rd Floor, Plot 3, Splendor Forum, Jasola District Centre, New Delhi – 110025, India

103 Penang Road, #05–06/07, Visioncrest Commercial, Singapore 238467

Cambridge University Press & Assessment is a department of the University of Cambridge.

We share the University's mission to contribute to society through the pursuit of education, learning and research at the highest international levels of excellence.

www.cambridge.org
Information on this title: www.cambridge.org/9781108411943

First published 2019

20 19 18 17 16 15 14 13 12 11 10 9 8 7 6 5

Printed in Poland by Opolgraf

A catalogue record for this publication is available from the British Library

ISBN 978-1-108-40531-7 Student's Book
ISBN 978-1-108-40509-6 Student's Book A
ISBN 978-1-108-40923-0 Student's Book B
ISBN 978-1-108-40532-4 Student's Book with Practice Extra
ISBN 978-1-108-40510-2 Student's Book with Practice Extra A
ISBN 978-1-108-40925-4 Student's Book with Practice Extra B
ISBN 978-1-108-40901-8 Workbook with Audio
ISBN 978-1-108-40874-5 Workbook with Audio A
ISBN 978-1-108-41194-3 Workbook with Audio B
ISBN 978-1-108-40518-8 Teacher's Edition with Test Generator
ISBN 978-1-108-41071-7 Presentation Plus
ISBN 978-1-108-41204-9 Class Audio CDs
ISBN 978-1-108-40795-3 Video Resource Book with DVD
ISBN 978-1-108-41449-4 Full Contact with DVD
ISBN 978-1-108-41155-4 Full Contact A with DVD
ISBN 978-1-108-41417-3 Full Contact B with DVD

Additional resources for this publication at www.cambridge.org/evolve

CONTENTS

UNIT 7 CAN WE TALK?

7.1 A COMMON LANGUAGE

1 VOCABULARY: Describing communication

A **Use the words in the box to describe the quotes. Sometimes there is more than one correct answer.**

catch up with	~~congratulate~~	criticize for
explain	gossip	keep in touch with
persuade to	reply	respond to

1 We were so excited to hear about the new baby. We're so happy for you!

congratulate

2 Well, I got a new job, and the baby is now walking! What's new with you?

3 Well, the reason that I was late was that my car broke down.

4 I just got your message. Yes, I will buy milk and bread.

5 Here are all the reasons we should get a dog.

6 Mike didn't do a great job on this report. He made several mistakes.

7 Hey. It's been a while since we talked, so I figured I'd call and say "hi."

8 Did you hear the news? Diana and Bernardo have broken up.

B **Circle the correct words to complete the sentences.**

1 No one *informed / contacted* me that the date of the party had changed.

2 Raquel was angry until Eduardo *gossiped / explained* that the reason he missed the party was that he was sick.

3 Julio didn't know about the hurricane until he saw it *reported / informed* on TV.

4 While we were catching up, Ben also *mentioned / recalled* that he got a new dog.

2 GRAMMAR: Reported speech

A **Read the conversation. Then circle the correct words. Sometimes both words are correct.**

Emma	I like your hat.
Amin	I have had it for a long time.
Emma	Well, it's very nice.
Amin	I've been ill.
Emma	I'm sorry to hear that.
Amin	I still don't feel well.

1 Emma *said / told* Amin that she *likes / liked* his hat.

2 Amin *said / told* that he *has / had had* it for a long time.

3 Emma *said / told* that it *is / was* very nice.

4 Amin *said / told* Emma that he is / *had been* ill.

5 Emma *said / told* that she *was / has been* sorry to hear that.

6 Amin *said / told* that he still *doesn't feel/ didn't feel* well.

B **Rewrite the sentences in reported speech.**

1 "I haven't gotten any messages in a week."

She said that she hadn't gotten any messages in a week.

2 "Sorry I'm late. I didn't know where to go."

He told us ______________________________.

3 "I haven't really kept in touch with Mike."

She said that ______________________________.

4 "I'm trying to persuade my husband to get a dog."

She told us that ______________________________.

5 "My boss criticized me for being late a couple times last week."

He explained that ______________________________.

6 "I don't recall having sent that email."

He claimed that ______________________________.

3 GRAMMAR AND VOCABULARY

A **Report what the people said. Replace *said* or *told* with one of the verbs in the box.**

commented ~~explained~~ informed persuaded recalled replied reported

1 "Jake needs to fill in two different forms," Risa said.

Risa explained that Jake needed to fill in two different forms.

2 "No, I haven't been able to contact Jane," Yumi said.

____

3 "The post is very funny," Victor said.

____

4 "There was an accident at your home in the morning," the police officer told Mr. Santiago.

____

5 "Take plenty of warm clothes on your trip," Sara told John. (He did what she said.)

____

6 Mike said, "In 1998, I saw the Statue of Liberty."

____

7 "You paid too much in taxes last year," the accountant said.

____

7.2 TO TEXT OR NOT TO TEXT

1 VOCABULARY: Talking about online communication

A **Complete the definitions with the words in the box.**

clickbait	geo-tag	hashtag	~~lurker~~	meme	newsfeed
podcaster	profile	status update	tag	timeline	trending topic

1 A ___lurker___ reads other people's comments and posts, but doesn't make their own comments or posts.
2 ________ is an article that is designed to get attention but that may not be true.
3 A ________ shows information about important things happening around the world.
4 You can find someone's photos and posts on their ________ .
5 A ________ is a piece of information (usually funny) that spreads very quickly on the Internet.
6 A ________ is something that a lot of people are currently posting about.
7 When you ________ a photo online, people know where the picture was taken.
8 When you post a ________ , you put new information online about yourself.
9 Your ________ has a description of you and your interests on a website.
10 When you ________ something online, you add information to it.
11 A ________ helps to connect an online post with other posts on the same topic.
12 If you are a ________ you host an online talk show.

2 GRAMMAR: Reporting questions

A **Put the words in the reported questions in the correct order.**

1 social media / asked / use / I / she / how often
She asked how often I use social media.
2 social media / asked / my parents / he / what / visited / sites / they
________ .
3 were / she / my favorite / what / blogs / asked
________ .
4 me / they / an iPad / used / if / asked / I / in high school / had
________ .
5 him / he / I / had / asked / met / if / anyone online
________ .
6 if / comment / asked / to / on / me / liked / videos / they / I
________ .

B **Write the direct questions from exercise 2A.**

1 *How often do you use social media?*
2 ______
3 ______
4 ______
5 ______
6 ______

3 GRAMMAR AND VOCABULARY

A **An interviewer asked Maria questions. Complete her answers with words from exercise 1A.**

1 Maria replied, "No, I never *tag* myself in my photos."
2 "I use ______ because more people see my ideas that way."
3 "I ______ my photos so people can see where I've been."
4 "I update my professional ______ every six months."
5 "No, I don't get all of my news from ______."
6 "My favorite ______ is Francine Veronica. I love her show."
7 "I often read about ______, since everyone is talking about them."
8 "I only share ______ that I think are funny and harmless."

B **Report the questions the interviewer asked.**

1 *The interviewer asked Maria if she ever tagged herself in her photos.*
2 ______
3 ______
4 ______
5 ______
6 ______
7 ______
8 ______

7.3 AND I'M LIKE ...

1 FUNCTIONAL LANGUAGE: Recounting stories

A **Complete the conversations. Use the phrases in the box.**

Apparently	~~I heard that~~	What happened was that
Who told you that	Wow, that's terrible	

Gloria So how was Tom's 30th birthday party? 1 ___I heard that___ Tom's brother, Steve, didn't go. 2 ______, he had the flu. He was too sick to get out of bed.

Hope 3 ______? That's all wrong. 4 ______ we had to change where the party was going to be. And anyway, nobody thought to call Steve and tell him. That's why he missed the party.

Gloria 5 ______!

in the end	it turns out that	someone told me that	was like	what happened was that

Ray Did you hear what happened to Ahsan last week?

Ivan 6 ______ he got fired for yelling at his boss.

Ray No, no, no. You see 7 ______ his boss told him he had to work over the weekend. And Ahsan 8 ______, "I can't. It's my daughter's birthday." Well, his boss told him that he had to work anyway, and Ahsan got mad and quit.

Ivan Really? Wow. That's too bad for Ahsan.

Ray Maybe not. You see, 9 ______ he was already thinking about looking for a new job. So, 10 ______ it might be for the best.

apparently	it turns out that	the funny thing is
you'll never believe this	what happened was	

Natasha Hey Vince. Did you hear about Sara?

Vince No. What?

Natasha 11 ______, but she got married last weekend!

Vince Get out of here! I didn't even know she was dating anyone.

Natasha 12 ______ she wasn't. 13 ______ she went to her high school reunion last month, and her old boyfriend was there. 14 ______ she still had feelings for him after all these years, and 15 ______ he felt the same way about her. So anyway, now they're married.

Vince Well good for them. I hope it works out.

2 REAL-WORLD STRATEGY: Getting back on track

A **Complete the conversation with the words in the box.**

I lost my train of thought	so, as I was saying	what was I saying	where was I? Oh yeah,

Irina Last night I couldn't get my daughter to put her tablet down.

Megan How is Olive? I heard that she won the swimming competition last week.

Irina Yeah. It was great. We were proud of her. Sorry, [1] ____________________ ? So she wouldn't put the tablet away, and I was getting really annoyed. I wanted her to help clean up, and she'd been chatting with her friend Julia for hours.

Megan I know exactly how you feel. Josh never helps clean up either.

Irina It's super frustrating, right? [2] ____________________ , she'd been chatting with her friend for hours and still wouldn't put the tablet away. So eventually, I took it and told her she couldn't have it back for a week.

Megan Ha! I'll bet that caused a fight.

Irina You better believe it. So she was yelling and screaming, and uh …

Megan Right, so she was yelling and screaming …

Irina Right. Sorry, [3] ____________________ . So anyway my husband comes in, like right in the middle of this, and gives her the tablet back! I couldn't believe it. I was so angry.

Megan I got angry with Mario last night. He was late for dinner, and I missed my meeting.

Irina That's too bad. So, [4] ____________________ David and I got into a big argument and now we're not talking to each other.

3 FUNCTIONAL LANGUAGE AND REAL-WORLD STRATEGY

A **Imagine you know the woman in the picture. Make up a story about what happened to her. Write a conversation telling a friend about it. Your friend interrupts at least one time. Begin like this:**

You *You'll never believe what happened to* ____________________

Friend ____________________

You ____________________

Friend ____________________

You ____________________

Friend ____________________

You ____________________

Friend ____________________

7.4 THE EMOJI CODE

1 READING

A **READ FOR MAIN IDEA** **Read the post. Underline the sentences that express the writer's main idea.**

Emojis | **Blog** | **Add comment** | **Share**

Are you someone like me who resists using emojis? Can you not understand why people prefer silly images over meaningful words? Well, I have news for you: You and I are the problem, not emojis. The world has moved on, and you and I must, too. Here's why:

Emojis are global. When people speak different languages, they find it hard to communicate. But emojis mean the same thing to everyone. It doesn't matter if they speak Chinese, English, or Spanish.

Emojis are a big part of social media. Emojis are all over social media. In some platforms, they are over 40% of text. In a few years, they will likely be over 50%. Future communication is certain to have more emojis and fewer words. People find emojis a simpler and faster way to communicate.

Emojis are part of our everyday lives. Now you can order pizza  with emojis in a Tweet. What will be next –  plane tickets? Why not?

Language changes slowly, but it is always happening. Emojis are part of today's change. They are here to stay, until the next change. 

B **READ FOR OPINIONS** **Read the post again. Circle the correct words to complete the statements.**

1 The writer believes that people who resist using emojis *have good reasons* / *are part of the problem.*

2 The writer says that emojis are *helpful* / *unhelpful* when people speak different languages.

3 The writer believes that emojis *may be* / *will definitely be* more common in the future.

2 LISTENING

A 7.01 **Listen to a discussion about using emojis in the classroom. Read the opinions. Write *G* for Gina's opinion, *K* for Ken's opinion, *B* for both, or *X* if something is not mentioned.**

1 Emojis improve communication. ___G___

2 Emojis help make creative work easier and more fun. ______

3 Students like what is familiar. That's why they prefer to use emojis to learn language. ______

4 Emojis can help with students who have clear communication difficulties. ______

5 Emojis can't help students understand difficult material like Shakespeare. ______

6 Just because students are interested doesn't mean they learn something well. ______

7 There are more benefits from using emojis for younger students than older ones. ______

8 There are many different kinds of activities students can do with emojis. ______

3 WRITING

A Write an informal email that does the following: tells the person you are going to miss a meeting, apologizes, and suggests a new time for the meeting.

B Now write a formal email that contains the same information from exercise 3A.

CHECK AND REVIEW

Read the statements. Can you do these things?

UNIT 7	Mark the boxes. ☑ I can do it. ? I am not sure. I can …	If you are not sure, go back to these pages in the Student's Book.
VOCABULARY	☐ use verbs and verb phrases to describe communication.	page 66
	☐ use terms for different types of online communication.	page 68
GRAMMAR	☐ report statements that were made in different tenses.	page 67
	☐ report questions that were asked in different tenses.	page 69
FUNCTIONAL LANGUAGE	☐ recount conversations, news, and stories.	page 70
	☐ get back on track after an interruption.	page 71
SKILLS	☐ write a formal and an informal email.	page 73

UNIT 8 LIFESTYLES

8.1 THE PERFECT JOB?

1 VOCABULARY: Describing jobs

A **Cross out the word that does not naturally follow the adjective.**

1 challenging:	work	day	job	~~vacation~~
2 high-paying:	position	employee	job	company
3 freelance:	company	job	position	worker
4 permanent:	career	employee	position	job
5 stressful:	boss	day	job	time
6 temporary:	job	friend	employee	place to live
7 tiring:	day	work	sleep	vacation
8 tough:	boss	job	fun	life

B **Complete the sentences. Use the words in the box.**

desk job	dream job	full-time job	~~government job~~
main job	part-time jobs	second job	

1 Teri is an accountant for the city of New York. She has a *government job*.
2 Magda wants to work 40 hours a week, but she can't find a __________. Instead, she's working two __________: one in a store for 15 hours a week and one in a restaurant for 20 hours a week.
3 Hector enjoys working with his hands and working outdoors. That's why he's so unhappy with his __________.
4 Suki's a high school teacher. That's her __________. But she needs more money, so she has a __________. She works in a restaurant on weekends and during summer vacation.
5 I love traveling and I love boats. So my __________ would be to work on a cruise ship and see the world.

2 GRAMMAR: Unreal present conditionals

A **Match 1–6 in column A with a–f in column B.**

A		B
1 If I didn't need the money,	*e*	a I might get a second job.
2 I'd invest in a new product if	___	b I'd be a great boss.
3 If I had a lot of free time,	___	c I wanted to work less.
4 I'd get together with friends more if	___	d I had money in the bank.
5 If I ran my own business,	___	e I wouldn't work two jobs.
6 I might take a salary cut if	___	f I weren't working all the time.

B **Put the words in order to form unreal conditional sentences.**

1 big house / if / I would / I lived / have / lots of space / in a

If I lived in a big house, I would have lots of space. OR I would have lots of space if I lived in a big house.

2 if / to the beach / didn't rain / more often / so much / it / we / would go

3 my neighborhood / always / so noisy / there / weren't / a lot of traffic / wouldn't be / if

4 far away / miss them / my family / lived / I / would / if

5 a dog / allergies / I would / didn't / if / get / I / have

3 GRAMMAR AND VOCABULARY

A **Write an unreal conditional sentence to show the opposite of each situation. Then write two more conditional sentences using the words from exercises 1A and 1B.**

1 I don't live in a big house. I don't have a lot of space.

If I lived in a big house, I would have a lot of space. OR I would have a lot of space if I lived in a big house.

2 My job is only part-time. I don't earn a lot of money.

3 My job is very challenging. I'm always tired when I get home.

4 My job is far away. It's not my dream job.

5 I don't work freelance. I am not my own boss.

6 I have a desk job. My job is very boring.

7

8

8.2 FINDING A BALANCE

1 VOCABULARY: Talking about work/life balance

A **Circle the correct answers.**

1 My family life is the *place I live* / *time I spend* with my family.
2 When you have me time, you *do things with others* / *relax on your own*.
3 When you have downtime, you *don't do very much* / *have a little time*.
4 If you have a 9 to 5 job, you spend most of the *day* / *night* in an office.
5 When you take time off, you are *doing* / *not doing* your usual work or studies.
6 At a seminar, a *large* / *small* group of people have a discussion with a teacher or expert.
7 Someone who is always connected can do things on *the Internet* / *a phone* all the time.
8 When you have an assignment, someone has given you work you *like to* / *have to* do.
9 If you have a busy schedule, you *have* / *don't have* a lot of free time.
10 When you work the *day* / *night* shift, you might work from 4 p.m. to midnight.
11 During a lecture, the professor speaks for *less* / *more* than ten minutes.
12 During office hours, professors often *talk to* / *test* their students.
13 When you have a busy social life, you spend a lot of time with your *co-workers* / *friends*.
14 When you have a commitment, you have something you *must* / *want to* do.

2 GRAMMAR: *I wish*

A **Read the sentences. Do they express present, past, or future wishes?**

1 I wish I had more time to study. *present*
2 I wish I hadn't bought these shoes. ______
3 I wish you hadn't moved away. ______
4 I wish I didn't have to work next week. ______
5 I wish I could go to the party tonight. ______
6 I wish you had told me the truth. ______
7 I wish I weren't living downtown. ______
8 I wish you were here. ______

B **Write the correct form of the verb in parentheses ( ).**

1 I wish I *could go* (can go) with you, but I have to stay home with the kids.
2 I wish I ______ (not buy) these shoes online. I don't like them, and I can't return them.
3 I wish I ______ (not take) the final exam next week. I need more time to study.
4 I wish I ______ (have) time to go to the party. I really don't want to miss it.
5 I wish I ______ (not have to) move. I know this apartment is small, but I really love it.
6 I wish I ______ (live) closer to my job. Then I could walk to work.
7 I wish I ______ (go) somewhere else for my vacation. It rained every day at the beach.
8 I wish I ______ (not say) that. It was rude. I'm sorry.

3 GRAMMAR AND VOCABULARY

A **Write sentences that are true for you. Use *wish* and the phrases in the box.**

(not) be always connected	have a (better) family life	have (more) time off
have a (more exciting) social life	~~have (more) downtime~~	(not) have a lot of commitments
(not) have a 9 to 5 job	take it easy (more)	(not) have a busy schedule
(not) work the night shift		

1 *I wish I had more downtime at work.*
2 ______
3 ______
4 ______
5 ______
6 ______
7 ______
8 ______
9 ______
10 ______

8.3 I WOULDN'T DO THAT!

1 FUNCTIONAL LANGUAGE: Discuss options

A **Match 1–8 in column A with a–h in column B.**

A		B
1 I would if	f	a I were you.
2 Have you	____	b you can do it next week?.
3 It can't	____	c you could offer to talk about the problem.
4 You might	____	d to lose.
5 Maybe	____	e tried talking to someone about the problem?
6 I'd try that if	____	f I were in your shoes.
7 You have nothing	____	g want to suggest another solution.
8 Is there anyway	____	h hurt, right?

2 REAL-WORLD STRATEGY: Negative advice

A **Correct the mistakes in the responses.**

1 A I'm going to leave my phone in the car.
B You don't want do that.
You don't want to do that.

2 A I'm going to stay home on the day of the exam.
B I couldn't do that if I were you!
____

3 A I'm going to complain to the boss about the job.
B You might to not want to do that.
____

4 A I'm going to lie to Sam about where I was last night.
B I'll avoid that if I were you.
____

5 A I'm going to tell my son that I don't like his new girlfriend.
B I wouldn't do that if I was you.
____

6 A I'm going to change my email password to 12345.
B I'd avoid that if I'd were you.
____

3 FUNCTIONAL LANGUAGE AND REAL-WORLD STRATEGY

A **Read the statements. Write advice.**

1 A I have real sleeping problems. Some nights I don't fall asleep for two hours.
B *Have you tried drinking warm milk? I've heard that helps.*

2 A My pants don't fit well. I'm not going to eat any bread, meat, or fruit until they fit again.
B *I wouldn't do that if I were you! A healthy diet includes all types of foods.*

3 A I can't believe I'm still living at home. I wish I could afford to get my own place.
B ____________________

4 A I can't seem to find a permanent job. For the past two years I've only gotten temporary ones.
B ____________________

5 A I have a 9 to 5 job that I really hate. I'm so bored that I want to quit.
B ____________________

6 A I've been working the night shift for two years. I've asked to work the day shift a few times, but I never get it.
B ____________________

7 A I'm going to take a trip around the world. I don't have much money, but I've heard it's not too hard to find work in other countries.
B ____________________

8 A I moved here six months ago and still don't know anyone. I'm lonely.
B ____________________

9 A I owe a friend some money, but I can't pay him back.
B ____________________

10 A A good friend of mine is depressed. I don't know what to do.
B ____________________

8.4 DIGITAL DETOX

1 LISTENING

A 8.01 **Listen to the conversation. What made Selena's digital detox successful?**

B 8.01 LISTEN FOR ATTITUDE **Listen again. Write *T* (true) or *F* (false) for each statement.**

1 Selena understands why Josh thinks she didn't enjoy her vacation. ____
2 Josh is surprised that Selena's digital detox worked. ____
3 Selena doesn't understand why Josh doubts the digital detox app. ____
4 At the end of the conversation, Josh changes his opinion of the digital detox app. ____

2 READING

A **Read the text. Check (✓) the benefits the writer mentions.**

The benefits of turning off your phone

A recent study has shown that we touch our phones 80 times a day on average. That is a shocking number, and it can't be good for us. Here are three ways turning off our phones can help us:

1. We are on our phones so much that we are filling our heads with unimportant information. We're not using our eyes to notice who and what is around us. Studies have shown that we get ideas from noticing things. If our brains are filled with unimportant things and not with new things we see around us, we have fewer new ideas.
2. People feel less stress when they stop using their phones all the time. They also sleep better. You certainly don't need your phone in your bedroom. Buy an old-fashioned alarm clock. It will do as good a job waking you up in the morning.
3. Having a conversation with someone is much better than 50 texts or 10 emails. This is especially true at work where co-workers get more things done and get them done faster when they talk face to face. People understand each other better and trust each other more.

1 Better education ☐
2 Better health ☐
3 Better ideas ☐
4 Better jobs ☐
5 Better relationships ☐

3 WRITING

A **Read the comments that listeners left on the podcast web page. Look at the underlined phrases. Then choose the correct answer.**

Comments

1 This week's podcast was really interesting. To be honest, I hadn't thought a lot about how often I use my phone. <u>As you said</u>, it's strange that my friends and I get together and then spend so much of the time looking at our phones. I have a question about where to go for digital detox. <u>You point out that</u> it is a good idea to go to a place where everybody is trying to do a digital detox. Does it matter if the people are friends or strangers? I mean, if a friend of mine wants to do a digital detox, could we go together or would that be a bad idea? I look forward to hearing your reply!

2 I really enjoyed this week's podcast. <u>There was one thing in particular that interested me.</u> I never knew there were places that focus on technology-free experiences. I was wondering if you could give me the names of two or three places like that.

These people use the underlined phrases to:

A give an opinion about what he or she heard in the podcast.

B refer to a statement or opinion he or she heard in the podcast.

B **Write a comment about the conversation you heard in exercise 1A. Use phrases that reference the speakers' statements or opinions.**

CHECK AND REVIEW

Read the statements. Can you do these things?

UNIT 8	Mark the boxes. ☑ I can do it. ? I am not sure. **I can …**	If you are not sure, go back to these pages in the Student's Book.
VOCABULARY	☐ **use adjectives to describe jobs and work situations.**	page 76
	☐ **discuss factors related to a healthy work/life balance.**	page 78
GRAMMAR	☐ **use present unreal conditionals.**	page 77
	☐ **express dissatisfaction with *I wish*.**	page 79
FUNCTIONAL LANGUAGE	☐ **discuss options.**	page 80
	☐ **offer a warning.**	page 81
SKILLS	☐ **write a comment about a podcast.**	page 83
	☐ **make reference to points other people make.**	page 83

UNIT 9 YES, YOU CAN!

9.1 READING THE SIGNS

1 VOCABULARY: Talking about places

A **Write the place under each picture. The first letter of each word is given to you.**

1 toll ______
plaza ______

2 r ______
a ______

3 b ______

4 c ______

5 p ______

6 c ______

7 c ______
s ______

8 r ______
s ______

9 l ______

B **Cross out the word that does not belong.**

1 Government buildings:	city hall	construction site	courthouse	consulate
2 City buildings:	arts center	city hall	consulate	rest stop
3 Outdoor areas:	boardwalk	laboratory	playground	public space

2 GRAMMAR: Prohibition, permission, obligation (present)

A **Circle the correct answer.**

1 You *aren't allowed to* / *aren't required to* wear shorts in the swimming pool.
2 You *are allowed to* / *are required to* have a passport for international travel.
3 You *are allowed to* / *are supposed to* arrive at the airport at least an hour before departure.
4 You *are supposed to* / *may not* use your phone during the exam. If you do, you will fail.
5 You *are allowed to* / *shouldn't* eat and drink during the break, but not during class.
6 You *may* / *must* leave the meeting early if you want to.

B **Complete the sentences. Use the verbs in parentheses ( ) and *(not) be allowed to*, *(not) be supposed to*, *(not) be required to*, or *may (not)*.**

1 There's a stop sign. You ___are required to stop___ (stop).
2 You ______________ (charge) your phone here. The sign says it's OK.
3 On the day of the exam, you ______________ (leave) your phone at home. If you don't, the teacher will take it away.
4 You ______________ (turn) right when the sign says "no right turn."
5 All students ______________ (take) the final exam. They can't pass the course without it.
6 I ______________ (be) here until 9 o'clock. I hope it's OK that I'm a little early.

3 GRAMMAR AND VOCABULARY

A **Write rules for each place. Use *(not) be allowed to*, *(not) be supposed to*, *(not) be required to* or *may (not)*.**

1 airport terminal (prohibition)
You are not allowed to go through security without a ticket.
2 boardwalk (permission)
____
3 city hall (obligation)
____
4 construction site (obligation)
____
5 courthouse (permission)
____
6 consulate (prohibition)
____
7 public space (permission)
____
8 residential area (prohibition)
____

9.2 RULES OF THE ROAD

1 VOCABULARY: Talking about rules

A **Write *N* if the underlined part of the sentence is a noun. Write *V* if it is a verb.**

1 Your car needs to be registered. V
2 Where's the registration? N
3 You are not permitted to park here. ______
4 There's a ban on noise after 11 p.m. ______
5 He lost control of the car and hit a tree. ______
6 The rule limits the number of cars. ______
7 There's a prohibition on smoking here. ______
8 Cars are banned from some parts of the downtown area. ______
9 You have my permission to go. ______
10 We are required to leave by 8. ______
11 I know my limits. ______
12 He is prohibited from entering. ______
13 It's your obligation to help. ______
14 Driving school isn't a requirement. ______
15 We are obliged to have a license. ______
16 Who controls the parking lot? ______

B **Complete the sentences with words from exercise 1A.**

1 Your life changes when you become a parent, because parents have many obligations .
2 There's a temporary ______ on soccer fans at the stadium. They are not allowed to attend any games.
3 There's a ______ on the number of students we can accept. This year we can't take more than 20.
4 Parents should ______ their children's behavior.
5 It is not a ______ to take English 1 before English 2, but it is a good idea.
6 Nobody is ______ to leave the building until the police say it is OK to do so.

C **Complete the sentences with your ideas.**

1 If I were the leader of my country, it would be a requirement for people to vote .
2 There should be a ban on ______ .
3 If I were the teacher, I would limit ______ .
4 I don't think children should be permitted to ______ .
5 I don't think governments should control ______ .
6 The prohibition against ______ should be removed.

2 GRAMMAR: Prohibition, permission, obligation (past)

A **Write the missing words.**

1 I ___could___ not play after school when I was young.

2 Victor was ________ to work last weekend, so he couldn't go to the game.

3 Were you allowed ________ eat candy when you were a child?

4 I ________ supposed to wear a suit at my last job, but sometimes I didn't.

5 The kids were ________ to play in the park until their parents came to get them. They always had fun.

6 Did you ________ to move, or did you move because you wanted to?

B **Write about the bike race Mario was in last month. Use *(not) allowed to, could (not), had to, supposed to,* and *required to.***

Rules of the Race

1 Mario ___was allowed to___ ride with a team.

2 Mario ________ stop another cyclist.

3 He ________ wear a helmet.

4 He ________ stop for water.

5 ________ have a second bike.

6 ________ cross the yellow line.

C **Rewrite the sentences. Use the words in parentheses ( ). Then check (✓) any sentences that used to be true in your country.**

1 It was a requirement for a child to start school at the age of 4. (require) ☐

A child was required to start school at the age of 4.

2 Students had to stand when the teacher entered the room. (require) ☐

____

3 It was necessary for students to wait until the teacher called on them before they spoke. (supposed to) ☐

____

4 Children could play in the streets until nighttime. (allow) ☐

____

5 A child couldn't talk when the family was having a meal. (allow) ☐

____

9.3 TO TIP OR NOT TO TIP?

1 FUNCTIONAL LANGUAGE: Making generalizations

A **Correct the mistakes in the sentences.**

1 I ~~general~~ generally don't eat a big breakfast.

2 I tend have just a cup of coffee.

3 On whole, mealtime isn't very important to me.

4 Generally speak, I don't eat dinner with my family.

5 In average, I eat with my family once or twice a week.

B **Complete the conversation. Sometimes there may be more than one answer.**

A Let me be the first one to say welcome to the company.

B Thank you. I'm really happy to be here.

A I know it's your first day, so do you have any questions?

B Uh, yeah a couple. Is there a dress code?

A 1 ______________________, no. You can dress pretty casually – unless we have a big meeting scheduled or something like that.

B That's good to know. What about start times? Do most people 2 ______________________ have a 9 to 5 schedule, or do some people start later or earlier?

A 3 ______________________, it's 9 to 5. But if there's a reason you need to work a different schedule, we can talk about it.

B No, 9 to 5 works fine for me. I was just curious. What about lunch? How much time do people take?

A 4 ______________________, about 30 minutes. Some people take a full hour and work a little later, though.

2 REAL-WORLD STRATEGY: Contrasting information

A **Read what speaker A says. Put the words in speaker B's response in the correct order. Which are true for you?**

1 **A** We tip 20% to a hairdresser.
B that / nearly / don't / much / tip / as / we / as
We don't tip nearly as much as that.

2 **A** Strangers shake hands when they meet.
B country / we / do / that / don't / in / it / way / my
____

3 **A** Friends kiss each other twice when they meet.
B really? / that / do / we / where / from / don't / come / I
____

4 **A** Workers get five weeks of vacation every year.
B back / differently / things / home / we / do
____

3 FUNCTIONAL LANGUAGE AND REAL-WORLD STRATEGY

A **Read Mathilde's comments about the French way of life. Respond with generalizations about your country.**

1 **Mathilde:** On average, French people work 35 hours a week.
On average, in Japan we work more than 40 hours a week.

2 **Mathilde:** On the whole, children in my region go to school four and a half days a week.
You: ______

3 **Mathilde:** Generally speaking, French people go on vacation in August.
You: ______

4 **Mathilde:** French people generally don't eat a sandwich for lunch.
You: ______

5 **Mathilde:** Young people tend to live with their parents until they're in their twenties.
You: ______

6 **Mathilde:** In general, French restaurants are open from noon to 2 p.m. and from 7 p.m. to 9 p.m.
You: ______

B **Check (✓) the generalizations about mealtime that are the same in your country. Write contrasting information for the sentences you do not check.**

1 We eat our main meal at noon. ☐
We do things differently back home. We eat our main meal at 6 in the evening.

2 In general, people eat cheese at the end of meals. ☐
______

3 We never have a meal without bread. ☐
______

4 Generally speaking, the whole family eats together on Sundays. ☐
______

5 Meals can last six hours. ☐
______

9.4 THE STORY OF THE RAMP

1 READING

A **Read the article. Who are Oscar and Mimi?**

When we think of animals that help disabled people, we usually think of dogs. They are great helpers to blind people and deaf people.

However, consider people in wheelchairs who can't use their arms or legs. They can't turn on the microwave oven or start up their computer. They can't pick up something that has fallen on the floor. Dogs can't help people who no longer have those abilities, but helper monkeys can.

That's why Oscar has Mimi. Oscar suffered serious injuries after a car accident and couldn't stay alone at home while his wife was at work; Mimi was the solution. She turns the TV on, switches the lights on and off, and brings Oscar something to drink when he is thirsty. The list of jobs around the house she can do is long. And the pleasure she gives Oscar is just as important. She hugs him. She sits on his leg and plays with him. He can't imagine life without her.

It takes three to five years to train a monkey to be comfortable in someone's home. They learn to respond to commands like "sun." That means "please turn on the light." They are trained to look for a laser light so that they know what the person they are helping wants. At the end of their training, they learn advanced skills like opening food containers and using different forms of technology.

With helper monkeys, people get back a lot of the independence and confidence they have lost. What's more, because monkeys live 30–40 years, they offer long-term companionship.

B **RECALL KEY INFORMATION** **Look at the questions. Can you remember the information? Check your answers in the article.**

1 Why can't Oscar use his arms and legs?
2 What are two things Mimi does for Oscar?
3 How long is the monkey's training?
4 How long do monkeys live?

2 LISTENING

A 9.01 **Listen to part of a talk show. Check (✓) the topic the people discuss. Do you agree with Vince or with Carla? Why?**

if people ever have trouble with their monkey helpers ☐
if monkey helpers get enough training ☐
if it is dangerous to have monkeys in people's home ☐
if it is right to use monkeys to help people ☐

3 WRITING

A Read the response to exercise 2A and circle the words that show the writer's attitude.

I have to say that I completely agree with Carla here. It's obviously important to help the disabled be as independent as possible, but we're forcing these monkeys to lead unnatural lives. Sadly, this is the case with many service animals. Frankly, I think it's very unfair the animals.

B **Do you agree or disagree with the use of service animals to help the disabled? Why? Use adverbs to show your attitude.**

CHECK AND REVIEW

Read the statements. Can you do these things?

UNIT 9	Mark the boxes. ☑ I can do it. ? I am not sure. **I can …**	If you are not sure, go back to these pages in the Student's Book.
VOCABULARY	☐ **use nouns and compound nouns to name different places.** ☐ **talk about rules.**	page 86 page 88
GRAMMAR	☐ **express prohibition, permission, and obligation in the present.** ☐ **express prohibition, permission, and obligation in the past.**	page 87 page 89
FUNCTIONAL LANGUAGE	☐ **use phrases to make generalizations.** ☐ **give contrasting information.**	page 90 page 91
SKILLS	☐ **express opinions in writing.** ☐ **use adverbs to show attitude.**	page 93 page 93

UNIT 10 WHAT IF ...?

10.1 ACCIDENTAL DISCOVERIES

1 VOCABULARY: Talking about discoveries

A **Match 1–9 in column A with a–i in column B.**

A

1 In their research, scientists noticed a __f__
2 They have been investigating the ____
3 They have been trying to gain ____
4 Scientists have faced ____
5 Studying frogs has provided ____
6 Researchers believe they have made a ____
7 Scientists have carried out ____
8 Nobody has been able to provide a ____
9 They are hoping to make ____

B

a phenomenon of frog behavior before bad weather.
b solution yet.
c important knowledge about predicting weather.
d breakthrough in understanding animal behavior.
e insights into how birds behave before storms.
f connection between weather and animal behavior.
g many challenges in doing this kind of research.
h an important discovery in the future.
i research into unusual animal behavior.

2 GRAMMAR: Past unreal conditionals

A **Read the situations. Then choose the sentence that explains the situation.**

1 We went out to eat because there was no food in the fridge.
   a We wouldn't have gone out to eat if there had been food in the fridge.
   b There would have been food in the fridge if we had gone out to eat.

2 Sylvia didn't go to the party because she had to work late.
   a If Sylvia had gone to the party, she wouldn't have had to work late.
   b If Sylvia hadn't had to work late, she would have gone to the party.

3 The forest fire started because someone at a campsite was careless.
   a If the forest fire hadn't started, someone at a campsite wouldn't have been careless.
   b If someone at a campsite hadn't been careless, the forest fire wouldn't have started.

4 George lost the race because he started one second late.
   a George wouldn't have lost the race if he hadn't started one second late.
   b George wouldn't have started one second late if he hadn't lost the race.

B **Put the words in the correct order to form sentences with unreal past conditionals.**

1 known / I / would / had / if / have / come / I

I would have come if I had known. OR If I had known, I would have come.

2 them / you / helped / asked / if / boys / have / the / had / would

3 more careful / fallen / been / you / you / if / had / have / wouldn't

4 we / the / been / sick / gone on vacation / have / baby / hadn't / if / would

5 you / if / would / seen you / the doctor / an appointment / earlier / have / made / had

6 you / you / would / had / I / me / texted / have / if / told

3 GRAMMAR AND VOCABULARY

A **Complete the sentences with the phrases in the box. Then rewrite the sentences with unreal past conditionals.**

a breakthrough	challenges	a connection	~~the phenomenon~~	research	a solution

1 Scientists didn't investigate _the phenomenon_ because they had no funding.

Scientists would have investigated the phenomenon if they'd had funding. OR If scientists had had funding, they would have investigated the phenomenon.

2 Scientists didn't notice ________ between cars and climate change because they didn't have enough information.

3 Researchers made ________ because they performed new experiments.

4 Scientists carried out new ________ because they didn't understand the problem.

5 It took years to complete the research because the researchers faced so many ________ .

6 Scientists were able to provide ________ because their research was successful.

10.2 BIG MISTAKE!

1 VOCABULARY: Discussing right and wrong

A **Do these sentences mean the same thing? Write *S* (same) or *D* (different).**

1 It was an epic fail.	It was a small mistake.	D
2 You'll have to correct the error.	You'll have to correct the mistake.	S
3 He blames me.	He says it's my fault.	______
4 It was a real blunder.	It was a big mistake.	______
5 I'll fix the problem.	I'll make it right.	______
6 There was confusion.	There was an error.	______
7 I got it wrong.	I made it right.	______
8 There was a mix-up.	There was a misunderstanding.	______
9 They didn't get it right.	They made an error.	______

2 GRAMMAR: Past modals

A **Complete the sentences. Use the words in parentheses ( ). Add *not* where necessary.**

1. Why didn't you tell me you were hungry? I *could have given* (could / give) you something to eat.
2. I wanted to go to the party, too. You ______________ (should / go) without me.
3. It's too bad you didn't take any medicine. It ______________ (might / help).
4. I'm sorry. I didn't know you needed money. I ______________ (could / lend) you some.
5. I didn't know you had a problem. You ______________ (should / call).
6. I told Charlie never to text and drive. He ______________ (might / have) the accident if he'd listened to me.
7. David was supposed to meet me at the station but he didn't. He ______________ (may / miss) his train.
8. Marta's computer was hacked. She ______________ (should / change) her password more often.

B **Write responses to the sentences in 1-8. Use *could, might,* and *should* and the words in the box.**

accept their job offer	fix it	get the position	have a good time
leave for work earlier	receive some gifts	walk	~~win~~

1 It's too bad you didn't run in the race.
You might have won. OR You could have won.

2 Why didn't you apply for the job?

3 It's too bad Araceli didn't come to the party.

4 It was a mistake not to take the other job.

5 It's too bad Josh was late for work.

6 Why didn't you tell us it was your birthday?

7 Why did you take the bus?

8 Why did they blame me for the problem?

3 GRAMMAR AND VOCABULARY

A **Complete the sentences with your own ideas.**

1 Maxine didn't correct the mistake until a month later.
She should have corrected it right away.

2 It wasn't your fault.
You couldn't ____________.

3 I couldn't fix the problem by myself. I should ____________.

4 I thought Martin told you the meeting had been canceled. It was a mix-up.
I should ____________.

5 Kara was to blame for the accident.
She shouldn't ____________.

6 It was an epic fail.
I might ____________.

7 It was a mistake to invite only some of my co-workers to the party.
I should ____________.

8 There was a lot of confusion about where to meet.
I should ____________.

10.3 YOU'LL NEVER GUESS!

1 FUNCTIONAL LANGUAGE: Engaging listeners

A **Circle the correct words.**

1 You won't *believe / think* this, but our flight was canceled.
2 Well, you *can / do* imagine. We were really upset.
3 Yeah, but you know *how / what*? We ended up getting free plane tickets.
4 *Are you / Do you get* ready for this?
5 They upgraded us to first-class seats. *Is / Isn't* that amazing?
6 We went out to look for the dog, and *don't / wouldn't* you know it? He was in the backyard the whole time.
7 So I found $100 on my way to the interview. But that's not *it / all*! I got the job, too!

2 REAL-WORLD STRATEGY: Showing interest in a story

A **Complete the conversation with the expressions in the box.**

Let me guess – you	~~Don't tell me you~~	You must be joking.	That's so awful

A My boss is really angry at me.
B 1 Don't tell me you were late for work again!
A Yup. That's the third time this month.
B 2 __________ forgot to set your alarm clock.
A No, I set it. But the power went out in the middle of the night and reset it.
B 3 __________. You have the worst luck.
A Yeah, tell me about it. Anyway, I tried to explain, but my boss said if it happens again he'd fire me.
B 4 __________. What are you going to do?
A Get to work on time! What else can I do?

3 FUNCTIONAL LANGUAGE AND REAL-WORLD STRATEGY

A **Complete the conversation with the expressions from exercises 1A and 2A.**

Ari You're back from your vacation. You look great! How was the hotel where you stayed?

Dia We never got there. You'll never [1] *guess what happened* .

Ari What?

Dia We rented a car at the airport. You won't [2] ________________ , but twenty minutes after we left the airport, we got a flat tire.

Ari Seriously? A flat tire on a rented car?

Dia We weren't happy. You can imagine. Anyway, while we were trying to change the tire, a man from the island stopped and asked if we needed help. By the time he changed the tire, it was lunchtime, so he invited us to have lunch with his family.

Ari Don't [3] ________________ you went to a stranger's home for lunch!'

Dia Everyone in the family was so friendly. They were happy to have us for lunch. Their home was next to the beach. [4] ________________ ? They had an extra room, and we ended up staying there.

Ari You must [5] ________________ ! The whole week?

Dia Yeah. The whole week. Isn't [6] ________________ ? The funny thing is we didn't need the car at all. We never went anywhere else on the island.

B **Imagine you are Dia. Something else surprising happened during the vacation. Write the conversation with expressions from exercises 1A and 2A. Use an idea in the box or your own idea.**

You took the wrong suitcase at the airport.	A famous person was at the beach every day.
Your flight home was canceled.	

Dia *You'll never guess what else happened to me.*

Ari ________________

Dia ________________

Ari ________________

Dia ________________

Ari ________________

Dia ________________

Ari ________________

10.4 I CAN'T LIVE WITHOUT IT!

1 LISTENING

A 10.01 **Listen to a conversation. What things do the man and woman agree they could not live without?**

B 10.02 LISTEN FOR TONE **Listen to the tone of the speakers' voices. Circle the correct answers.**

1 "You mean like air, food, and water?"
  (a) She is trying to be funny.
  b She wants information.
2 "Paper and pen?"
  a She is asking if he needs paper and a pen.
  b She is surprised.
3 "I just love them."
  a He is saying a fact.
  b He is not serious.
4 "Really, I couldn't live without either of my parents."
  a He is saying a fact.
  b He is trying to be funny.
5 "Sunsets at the beach?"
  a She is asking him to repeat the question.
  b She is surprised.

2 READING

A **Read the story. What did Olivia learn about living without the things she had loved before?**

When Olivia Stanton lost her job, she seemed to have lost everything. First it was her apartment and all the things she couldn't take when she moved in with her sister. There was her piano, her furniture, and the books she loved. The only thing she kept with her the whole time was her laptop computer. Without the computer, she wouldn't have been able to look for a job or stay in touch with friends.

For the first few months, Olivia found it very hard to live without all of her things. But as time went on, she learned she actually enjoyed life more with less stuff. She started looking for other things she could live without. She got rid of her car and started walking more or taking the bus. She gave up her gym membership and started running in the park instead.

She also started a blog about her new stuff-free lifestyle. From that blog, she got an offer to write a book and a $10,000 advance. With the $10,000, Olivia has been able to re-establish her life. She moved out of her sister's house and got a new apartment – a smaller one that fits with her new lifestyle. She has no desire to get back all the things she had before. Aside from the laptop, she has found that the only things she can't live without are her friends and the opportunities she found online.

B **Circle the correct answers.**

1 Olivia moved out of her apartment (*after*) / *before* she lost her job.
2 Olivia got rid of most of her things *when she moved to her sister's* / *because she needed the money.*
3 Olivia found that without all of her things life got *better* / *worse.*
4 Olivia was able to get a new apartment because she got a *new job* / *an offer to write a book.*

3 WRITING

A **Read the post from Olivia's blog. Circle the words that show contrast and underline the words that show similarity.**

When I think about my old lifestyle, it really couldn't be more different from how I live now. My life was full of things. I mean, I owned a lot of stuff, but the things I owned didn't really make me happy. I had a nice car, but I was always worried it would get scratched or dented whenever I drove somewhere. Similarly, I had a lot of really nice clothes, but I worked so much to afford them that I never had time to wear the outfits I liked so much. Now, on the other hand, I have a lot fewer things. But the things I do own are things I truly enjoy, and I also have time to actually enjoy them now.

B **Write a comment about what is and is not important in your life. Use the words from exercise 3A to help you.**

CHECK AND REVIEW

Read the statements. Can you do these things?

UNIT 10	Mark the boxes. ☑ I can do it. ? I am not sure. I can …	If you are not sure, go back to these pages in the Student's Book.
VOCABULARY	☐ **use verb + noun phrases to describe research, investigation, and discovery.**	page 98
	☐ **talk about right and wrong.**	page 100
GRAMMAR	☐ **use past unreal conditionals to discuss present outcomes.**	page 99
	☐ **use modals of past probability to suggest unreal alternative outcomes.**	page 101
FUNCTIONAL LANGUAGE	☐ **keep a listener engaged.**	page 102
	☐ **show interest in a story.**	page 103
SKILLS	☐ **write a comment on a blog post.**	page 105
	☐ **use words to show similarity and contrast in writing.**	page 105

UNIT 11 CONTRASTS

11.1 STUDENT STORIES

1 VOCABULARY: Talking about college education

A **Use the words in the box to complete the email from a college student in his first week.**

association	~~campus~~	degrees	dorm	facilities	faculty	freshmen
grades	majors	professors	semester	society	undergraduate	

Hi Sis!

I just wanted to write quickly and let you know how things are going here. So far, everything's great! The [1] ___campus___ is really beautiful, but it's also huge. I've gotten lost a couple times. The [2] ______________ I'm staying in is nice and modern, and my roommate seems like a nice guy. I think we'll get along really well. There was a meeting for all the [3] ______________ last night. It was a good chance to meet people since we're all new here. A couple members of the [4] ______________ were there also, although I won't meet any of my [5] ______________ until classes start on Monday.

The [6] ______________ here are fantastic! The cafeteria is big and has great food. There's a gym and a swimming pool.... There's even a library just for [7] ______________ students. People studying for advanced [8] ______________ apparently have a separate library.

I think I'm going to have a lot of fun this [9] ______________. I've already joined an acting [10] ______________. But don't worry, I'm not going to neglect my studies or let my [11] ______________ fall. I've also joined an [12] ______________ for engineering [13] ______________, so I'll have plenty of study partners.

Anyway, gonna go now. Miss you lots,

Roberto

2 GRAMMAR: Gerund and infinitive after *forget*, *remember*, *stop*

A **Check (✓) the correct sentences. Then correct the mistakes in the incorrect sentences.**

1 I'll never forget climbing that mountain. It was so exciting. ☑

2 Do you remember ~~to see~~ *seeing* my phone anywhere? ☐

3 You forgot texting me again. Why can't you remember? ☐

4 I stopped buying some milk. Here it is. ☐

5 I stopped playing video games a few years ago. I was playing them too much. ☐

6 Sorry. I didn't remember bringing your book. I'll bring it tomorrow. ☐

7 I remember meeting the owner of the business, but I can't remember his name. ☐

8 I stopped at the ATM machine to get some money. ☐

B **Complete the conversations. Use the words in parentheses ( ).**

1 **A** I can't find my phone.
B I ___remember seeing___ (remember / see) you with it a short time ago.

2 **A** I didn't tell Anita and Diego about the party.
B I'll ____________ (remember / tell) them later on.

3 **A** I'm going out now.
B Don't ____________ (forget / get) something for dinner.

4 **A** What is something you will never forget?
B I'll never ____________ (forget / meet) my wife for the first time.

5 **A** Are these flowers for me?
B Yes, I ____________ (stopped / buy) them for you on my way home from work.

6 **A** Are you a vegetarian?
B Yes, I ____________ (stopped / eat) meat when I was in high school.

3 GRAMMAR AND VOCABULARY

A **Complete the conversations using the words in the box and the words in parentheses ( ).**

campus	dorm	facilities	grades	professor	semester	society

1 **A** Thank goodness! My ____________ are finally improving.
B That's great. What are you doing differently?
A I ____________ (stop, play) so many video games.

2 **A** Did you finish your research paper?
B What paper? I ____________ (not, remember, have) a paper due this week!
A Well, we have one. The ____________ assigned it a month ago.

3 **A** So are you joining the theater ____________?
B No. I ____________ (forgot, sign up) by the deadline.
A That's too bad. Well maybe you can join next ____________.

4 **A** Well, I'm back from my tour of the college.
B Did you ____________ (remember, ask) about the gym and the swimming pool?
A Yeah, we saw them. They're really nice ____________.

5 **A** Did you live in a ____________ in college?
B At first. But I had the messiest roommate. He never cleaned up. I couldn't take it. I had to ____________ (stop, live) with him and move into an apartment just off ____________.

11.2 FOLK REMEDIES

1 VOCABULARY: Talking about science

A **Complete the sentences with the correct words in the box.**

science scientist scientific ~~scientifically-proven~~

1 Something that is *scientifically-proven* has been studied for a long time.
2 Chemistry is my favorite type of ____________________ .
3 Chris likes to read books about ____________________ subjects.
4 Have you always wanted to be a ____________________ ?

research (*n.*) researcher research (*v.*) research-based

5 ____________________ studies can take many years to complete.
6 ____________________ shows that sleep is necessary.
7 The ____________________ talked about the results of her study.
8 We have to ____________________ how to solve the problem.

proof prove proven scientifically-proven

9 Ginger is a ____________________ remedy for an upset stomach. Research has been done about it.
10 You have to ____________________ your ideas.
11 What ____________________ do you have?
12 This is a ____________________ fact.

base (*n.*) basis base (*v.*) based scientifically-based

13 The report is ____________________ on research from three different universities.
14 What is the ____________________ of the study?
15 Students need a good ____________________ in mathematics.
16 You should ____________________ your research on children between the ages of 8 and 14.
17 All of the information is ____________________ . The research took place over 10 years.

medicine medical medically-approved

18 The ____________________ exercises are helping my back pain. I should thank my doctor for showing them to me.
19 Do you like looking at ____________________ websites?
20 My cousin is majoring in ____________________ . She wants to be a doctor.

2 GRAMMAR: *help, let, make*

A **Circle the correct words. Sometimes more than one word is correct.**

1 We have a really furry dog, so we don't *help* / *let* / *make* him sit on the couch.
2 Warm milk *helps* / *lets* / *makes* me sleep.
3 Some kinds of music *help* / *let* / *make* me want to dance.
4 Snakes *help* / *let* / *make* a lot of people feel frightened.
5 Interesting activities *help* / *let* / *make* students learn.
6 Please be quiet and *help* / *let* / *make* the teacher speak.

B **Complete the sentences. Use *help, let,* or *make* and the correct pronoun.**

1 **A** Does your mother ever feel sleepy when she watches TV?
B Yes, watching TV makes her feel sleepy.
2 **A** Why do you listen to that loud music?
B It ______________ relax.
3 **A** Do you stay out late at night?
B Yes, my parents ______________ stay out late.
4 **A** Did you have to do a lot of chores as a child?
B Of course. Our parents ______________ clean the house every Saturday.
5 **A** Can you please turn off the computer?
B It won't ______________ shut it down. It must be broken.

3 GRAMMAR AND VOCABULARY

A **Answer the questions. Try to use the words from exercise 1A in your answers.**

1 What's something that helps scientists conduct research?
____
2 What can doctors do to make people trust them more?
____
3 Should we let people take medicines that aren't medically-approved?
____
4 What is a popular belief that is not scientifically-based?
____

11.3 CAN YOU SUGGEST AN ALTERNATIVE?

1 FUNCTIONAL LANGUAGE: Discussing alternatives

A **Complete the conversation. Use the words from the box.**

also	alternative	another	~~can~~	else	great
is	like	might	that	work	

Customer Hello. I'm looking for a book for my 12-year-old nephew.

Bookseller This book has always worked well with boys of that age.

Customer [1] ___Can___ you suggest an alternative? My nephew doesn't like sports very much.

Bookseller You could [2] ________ try this book. It's very popular with boys and girls.

Customer It [3] ________ not be the best option. He could think it's for girls. [4] ________ there something different?

Bookseller Don't worry. We have plenty of books for that age group. [5] ________ option would be this book about famous people in history.

Customer That could [6] ________ . Do you have anything [7] ________ ?

Bookseller I also have these books on the animal world. They're a good [8] ________ .

Customer Hmm. I don't think they're a [9] ________ choice. He's never shown an interest in animals.

Bookseller Then how about these comic books? They're very interesting. Boys love them.

Customer That looks [10] ________ a good alternative.

Bookseller I also have these funny novels. They make kids laugh a lot.

Customer I like [11] ________ option, too. Now I have to decide which is better. It's not an easy choice!

2 REAL-WORLD STRATEGY: Giving a personal recommendation

A **Complete the conversations with personal recommendations. Use your own ideas.**

1 **A** I've been trying to lose weight but nothing seems to work. What would you suggest?
  B ________ has always worked for me.

2 **A** I'm thinking of buying a new car. What do you think I should get?
  B If I were you, ________ .

3 **A** I spilled pasta sauce all over this shirt. What should I use to get the stain out?
  B I've always had good luck with ________ .

4 **A** I have some vacation time coming up. Where do you think I should go?
  B ________

5 **A** It's my wife's birthday next week. Where do you think I should take her for dinner?
  B ________

3 FUNCTIONAL LANGUAGE AND REAL-WORLD STRATEGY

A **Nicolas is in a jewelry store talking to Carla, the store owner. Follow the instructions in parentheses ( ) to complete the conversation. Use the expressions in exercises 1A and 2A.**

Nicolas I'm looking for a gift for my girlfriend.

(Carla recommends a bracelet.)

Carla 1 If I were you, I'd choose a bracelet. How about one of these?

(Nicolas likes that suggestion. Then he asks for options.)

Nicolas 2 ______ But I was looking for something more elegant. 3 ______

(Carla suggests earrings as an alternative.)

Carla We have some beautiful necklaces. 4 ______

(Nicolas discusses the disadvantage of earrings.)

Nicolas 5 ______ My girlfriend doesn't wear earrings very often.

(Carla suggests the option of a matching bracelet and necklace.)

Carla 6 ______

(Nicolas responds to the suggestion.)

Nicolas 7 ______

(Carla recommends another bracelet and necklace.)

Carla 8 ______ The bracelet and necklace can be worn separately, or the bracelet can be attached to the necklace to make it longer. That way you have two necklaces.

(Nicolas likes that option.)

Nicolas 9 ______ I'll take it.

11.4 DRIVERLESS CARS? NO WAY!

1 READING

A **Read the article. Is the writer for or against driverless cars?**

People rarely like change. They find it frightening. Technology introduces something new, and people say they don't want it or need it.

How do you feel about riding in an elevator? You are probably comfortable. Can you imagine people ever being against an elevator? That is exactly what happened when elevators first appeared. At first, it was someone's job to operate the elevator. People on the elevator just had to get used to going up and down. But when elevators became automatic, people did not like the change at all. There was no human in control. People were scared to let a machine do everything.

So what happened? People got used to elevators. A soft voice gave instructions. There was relaxing music to calm the riders. Now it has been more than 150 years since the invention of the elevator, and people are against another invention: the driverless car. I hear my friends saying things like, "How will I be in control? The car will do anything it wants!"

The fact is that driverless cars will probably be safer than cars driven by human beings. People sometimes fall asleep at the wheel. They get distracted by their phones or by other passengers. And some people are just not very good drivers. With a driverless car, all of these problems disappear.

In the end, I predict the driverless car will become just like the elevator. People will be just as comfortable in a driverless car as they are in an elevator that is moving them from the first to the twenty-first floor.

B **IDENTIFYING ARGUMENTS** **Read the article again. Check (✓) the arguments the writer uses to support her opinion.**

1 New technology is frightening. ☐
2 People did not like elevators but eventually got used to them. ☐
3 Driverless cars are unsafe for small children and the elderly. ☐
3 People are already unsafe drivers, and driverless cars will be safer. ☐
4 Driverless cars will be much more comfortable than driving ourselves. ☐

2 LISTENING

A 🔊 11.01 **Listen to the conversation. Write *T* (true) or *F* (false).**

1 The woman wants a driverless car. ______
2 The man will never want a driverless car. ______
3 The man likes to drive. ______
4 The woman doesn't think driverless cars are safer. ______

3 WRITING

A **Read the comment in response to the article. Circle the transition phrase that starts an opinion. Underline the transition phrases that add to the opinion. Draw a box around the transition phrase that ends the opinion.**

I'm not a car lover. I drive only because I have to. That doesn't mean I love the idea of driverless cars.

First of all, driverless cars are really just computers on wheels. Computers are hacked all the time. What will prevent a hacker somewhere in the world from getting control of my car? More importantly, what will stop other people from making my car do dangerous things? It's also important to remember that driverless cars are programmed to drive on the road. What if there is an emergency and I need to drive off the road, perhaps into a field? Additionally, human drivers know that when they see a plastic bag on the road, it is not dangerous. A driverless car might not know that and might try to avoid it. That could cause an accident. Finally, think of all the people who will lose their jobs if drivers are no longer needed. What will happen to them?

B **Write a response to the article in exercise 1A. Give your opinion about driverless cars. Use the correct transition phrases.**

____

____

____

____

____

____

CHECK AND REVIEW

Read the statements. Can you do these things?

UNIT 11	Mark the boxes. ☑ I can do it. ? I am not sure. **I can …**	If you are not sure, go back to these pages in the Student's Book.
VOCABULARY	☐ **use words to talk about college life.** ☐ **use different word forms to discuss science and medicine.**	page 108 page 110
GRAMMAR	☐ **change meaning by using gerunds or infinitives after *forget*, *remember*, and *stop*.** ☐ **use causative verbs *help*, *let*, and *make* to indicate effects caused by someone or something else.**	page 109 page 111
FUNCTIONAL LANGUAGE	☐ **discuss alternatives.** ☐ **give a personal recommendation.**	page 112 page 113
SKILLS	☐ **write a comment in response to an article.** ☐ **use transition phrases to add to and conclude arguments.**	page 115 page 115

UNIT 12 LOOKING BACK

12.1 PHOTO STORIES

1 VOCABULARY: Talking about the senses

A **Match the descriptions in column A with the adjectives in column B.**

A		B
1 the way a piece of cake should taste	*e*	a bright
2 the way a baby's cheek feels	____	b colorful
3 the way a song can sound	____	c damp
4 the way old books can smell	____	d deep
5 the way a man's voice can sound	____	e flavorful
6 the way a small child's voice can sound	____	f fresh
7 a day when the sun is shining	____	g high-pitched
8 the way a wet towel can smell	____	h melodic
9 the way the skin of a lemon feels	____	i musty
10 the way grass can smell after it rains	____	j rough
11 a shirt that is orange, yellow, green, and blue	____	k smooth

B **Write sentences about what you like and don't like. Use the adjectives in exercise 1A and the nouns in the box, or your own ideas.**

clothes	faces	fish	fruit	meals	music	rooms
soap	socks	sounds	summer days	~~voices~~	weather	wool

1 *In my opinion, long beards are a fad. I don't think they'll be popular next year.*
2 ____
3 ____
4 ____
5 ____
6 ____

2 GRAMMAR: Adding emphasis

A **Check (✓) the sentences that add emphasis to an idea. Then underline the words that add emphasis.**

1 <u>What I do in my free time</u> is not your concern. ☑
2 The thing I like most about my job is the money. ☐
3 What do you remember most about elementary school? ☐
4 The thing I love about my home is the light. ☐
5 What I don't want is another problem with my car. ☐
6 What do you mean when you say you don't understand? ☐

B **Complete the sentences. Use the words in parentheses ( ). Write two sentences with your own ideas.**

1 The *thing I like most about Florida is* the weather. (I like most about Florida)
2 What ______ the noise. (bothers me a lot)
3 What ______ a vacation. (I need)
4 What ______ her name. (I can never remember)
5 What ______ my children's health. (worries me all the time)
6 The ______ saying goodbye. (I hate the most)
7 What ______ science fiction novels. (I really like to read)
8 The ______.
9 What ______.

3 GRAMMAR AND VOCABULARY

A **Answer the questions. Add emphasis to your ideas. Try to use the words from exercise 2B in your responses.**

1 What was the thing you most liked to eat when you were a child?
The thing I most liked to eat was a banana.
2 What do you like the most about your home?
______
3 What do you want most of all in the future?
______
4 What is something you love doing on the weekend?
______
5 What do you dislike the most about your town?
______
6 What is the thing you enjoy the most on social media?
______

12.2 DID THAT REALLY HAPPEN?

1 VOCABULARY: Describing memories

A **Write the word that matches the definition.**

bring back	childhood	~~clear~~	distant	early
long-term	look back on	recall	recent	recognize
remind someone of	short-term	vague	vivid	

1 describing memories that are easy to see in your mind *clear*
2 describing memories or events that happened a short time ago ________
3 describing memories that stay in your mind for a lot of time ________
4 describing memories that produce strong images in your mind ________
5 describing memories that are temporary ________
6 describing memories or events that happened a long time ago ________
7 describing memories that are not complete or uncertain ________
8 the part of your life when you were young ________
9 describing some of the first memories you have ________
10 to know people or places because you have seen or experienced them before ________
11 to think about a time in your past ________
12 to make someone think of someone or something else ________
13 to remember a fact or event ________
14 to make someone think about something from the past ________

B **Complete the sentences with words from exercise 1A. Don't use the same word twice. Then rewrite the sentences so that they are true for you.**

1 The thing I *recall* most about my childhood is my family's farm.
The thing I recall most about my childhood is playing with my brother and sister.

2 When I ________ my childhood, I get sad.

3 Going back to my old neighborhood ________ me of the past.

4 I have very ________ memories of my grandparents. It's like they are still here with me.

5 Getting together with all my cousins ________ wonderful memories.

6 I have a ________ memory of my first school. I remember the outside but not the classrooms.

2 GRAMMAR: Substitution and referencing

A **Complete the sentences. Use the words in the boxes.**

~~it~~ one ones them

1 If we don't have your email address, please send ___it___ .
2 If these videos don't interest you, tell us the ______ you would like to see.
3 If you don't have a teacher, we will find you ______ .
4 I got you these books. I hope you like ______ .

did do not so

5 Do you want to learn more? If ______ , please write us today.
6 I didn't learn anything, but other people ______ .
7 Are you going to do the required work? If ______ , we can't help you.
8 I don't have a lot of free time, but they ______ .

B **Underline the words that are repeated. Then replace the underlined words.**

1 If you don't remember the number, I can give the number (it) to you.
2 Do you want to improve your memory? If you want to improve your memory, read this.
3 My brother doesn't remember our childhood well, but I remember.
4 I played with my cousins on Sundays. I got together with my cousins at my grandparents' home.
5 I don't recall a pink house, but I remember a green house.
6 Does Hilda remember? If Hilda doesn't remember, ask Nick.

C **Look at the sentences with substitutions or referents. Write the sentences that come before them. Use your own ideas.**

1 ___Are you going to do the dishes?___ If not, I'll do them.
2 ______ I have brown ones.
3 ______ , but I did. I went often.
4 ______ I felt bad because I was the only one who didn't.
5 ______ , but I do.
6 ______ If so, let me know.

12.3 THAT RINGS A BELL

1 FUNCTIONAL LANGUAGE: Recalling past experiences

A **Correct five mistakes in the conversation.**

Natalia I love this picture.

Greg Where was that taken?

Natalia Don't ~~say to~~ tell me you don't remember the high school picnic.

Greg Which picnic?

Natalia The picnic when it started to rain.

Greg Oh yeah. That rings. We all ran under a tree. That was really dumb.

Natalia Well, are you remembering the time it started to rain at the soccer game?

Greg No. I didn't recall rain at a soccer game. Are you sure I was there?

Natalia Absolutely. You were the only one who had an umbrella. We all tried to get under it.

Greg Yeah. It all comes back to me now. That was funny!

2 REAL-WORLD STRATEGY: Sharing experiences

A **Complete the conversation. Use the phrases in the box.**

had a similar experience	of a story	that ever happened	that's like the time

Luis Once I was fishing. I took off my watch and it fell in the lake. That was the end of that watch! Has [1] ____________________ to you?

Renée Well, I haven't lost anything in a lake, but that reminds me [2] ____________________ . [3] ____________________ that I lost my glasses. I'd put them on the top of the car. I started driving. Then I realized I wasn't wearing my glasses. When I got out of the car, they weren't there anymore.

Joel You know, I [4] ____________________ once, but in my case I had left my house keys on top of the car. When I got home, I had to break the window to get into the house.

3 FUNCTIONAL LANGUAGE AND REAL-WORLD STRATEGY

A **Read the stories. Then complete the conversation. Use the facts in the stories and your own ideas.**

Amanda and Ron took a bike trip with other friends a few years ago. One day they were in a village. A dog ran across the road right in front of Amanda. She tried to avoid hitting the dog and fell off the bike. She couldn't get up because she was in a lot of pain. Some villagers came to help her. One of them took her to the local hospital. Her friends rode their bikes there. It was a very small hospital. It turned out she had broken her arm and couldn't continue on the bike trip.

Manuel once fell off a horse when he was on vacation. He'd been riding the horse when something scared it. The horse threw Manuel off and ran away. At first, Manuel's shoulder hurt him, but he was OK. He was able to walk and found the horse about a mile down the road.

Amanda Do you remember that time ______ *I broke my arm on the bike trip?*

Ron That trip's a bit vague for me. ______

______

Amanda Don't tell me you don't remember, Ron. ______

______

Ron Oh yeah, that rings a bell. ______

Amanda ______

______

Ron Yeah, it's all coming back to me now. ______

______ Has that ever happened to you, Manuel?

Manuel That reminds me of a story, but not with a bike. That's like the time that ______

______

Ron You know, I had a similar experience once with a horse. ______

______

12.4 MAN'S BEST FRIEND?

1 LISTENING

A 12.01 **Listen to the conversation. Answer the questions.**

1 Who are Lily and Chelsea?

2 What does the woman dislike about Dan's dog?

3 According to Dan, how does the dog show happiness?

4 According to Vic, what does Dan do that is dangerous?

B 12.01 LISTEN FOR EXAMPLES **Listen again. Put the words and phrases from the conversation in the order that you hear them. Then check (✓) whether they are transitions to change from one topic to another or examples to support an argument.**

		Transition	Example
____	The thing is	☐	☐
____	like (jumping)	☐	☐
____	In fact	☐	☐
____	I mean … just think about	☐	☐
____	For instance	☐	☐
1	Actually	☑	☐

2 READING

A **Read advice for training a dog. Then choose the best title for each piece of advice.**

Dog training | Contact us | Reviews

____

There's nothing a dog likes more than food. When you're training your dog, always have something in your pocket to reward the dog's good behavior. This way the dog will repeat the behavior. It's like you and your paycheck. You wouldn't go to work if you didn't get one. The treat your dog gets is like a paycheck. It makes the dog want to continue going "to work."

____

When you're in a public space, it's important to control your dog. That's why the dog must be trained not to leave your side. Start the training in your home. Dogs are usually taught to stay to the left, but it's OK if you prefer the right. When you give the dog a treat for good behavior, make sure it's from the hand next to the dog. You don't want it to go in front of you to get the treat. When the dog has gotten good in your home at not moving from your side, the dog is ready to continue its training outside.

a Make your dog want to come when you call

b Teach your dog to walk beside you

c Train your dog with something it loves

d Train your dog not to touch dangerous things

3 WRITING

A **Read a summary of an opinion about dog training classes. Underline contrasting ideas. Circle the words that link them.**

> The speaker argued that dog training classes should not be required. She claimed that many dogs still misbehave despite having had training. She argued that some types of dogs are just naturally more obedient, and that other types of dogs naturally resist training. Personally, I disagree. While it is true that some dogs are more naturally obedient, all dogs benefit from training, and there's not a dog that can't be trained with enough work.

B 🔊 12.01 **Listen again. Take notes on Vic's and Dan's arguments. Write a summary contrasting their opinions. Mention the points that you agree and disagree with. Conclude your summary with a general opinion.**

____

____

____

____

____

____

____

____

CHECK AND REVIEW

Read the statements. Can you do these things?

UNIT 12	Mark the boxes. ☑ I can do it. ? I am not sure. **I can …**	If you are not sure, go back to these pages in the Student's Book.
VOCABULARY	☐ **use sense adjectives for descriptions.** ☐ **use words to describe and share memories.**	page 118 page 120
GRAMMAR	☐ **emphasize something by using the structure *What I remember most is …* or *The thing I liked was … .*** ☐ **use substitution and referencing to avoid repetition.**	page 119 page 121
FUNCTIONAL LANGUAGE	☐ **recall a memory.** ☐ **share experiences.**	page 122 page 123
SKILLS	☐ **write a summary of an opinion.** ☐ **write about contrasting ideas.**	page 125 page 125

EXTRA ACTIVITIES

7.5 TIME TO SPEAK Online communication survey

A **Choose one of the online activities below or think of a different online activity.**

- online dating
- online shopping
- online gaming
- watching online videos
- listening to podcasts

B **Create a survey about the activity you chose. Think of four or five questions to ask about it. Give the survey to your family and friends or post it on one of your social media accounts.**

C **Bring the results to your next class. Explain your survey and present the results to the rest of the class.**

8.5 TIME TO SPEAK Planning a digital detox

A **Try a digital detox between now and your next class. What online activities are you willing to give up?**

- ☐ checking your social media accounts
- ☐ reading articles online
- ☐ watching videos online
- ☐ texting/messaging friends and family
- ☐ using apps on your phone

B **Make a digital detox plan to help you give up the activities you checked in A.**

C **In your next class describe your plan for a digital detox and report back to the class. Where you successful? Why or why not?**

9.5 TIME TO SPEAK Sell it!

A **Go online and research a technology, device, or service that helps people with a disability.**

- What is the technology, device, or service?
- What type of disability is it for?
- How does it help a disabled person?
- Who pays for it? (the disabled person, the government, a charity, …)

B **Write a summary of the technology, device, or service you researched.**

C **Bring the summary to your next class. Explain the technology, device, or service to the class.**

10.5 TIME TO SPEAK Turning points

A **Think of the kinds of events that can change people's lives completely (a turning point). Think of a friend or family member who has had an interesting turning point in his/her life. Make a video asking the person about the turning point, or go online and find someone talking about a turning point in his/her life.**

B **Bring the video to your next class. Explain how the person's life would be different if the turning point had not happened.**

11.5 TIME TO SPEAK Mediation

A **Think of a time you mediated a disagreement between co-workers or friends.**

- What was the disagreement about?
- What solution did you suggest?
- Were both people happy with the solution you suggested? Why or why not?

B **In your next class, describe the disagreement and the solution you suggested.**

12.5 TIME TO SPEAK Where were you when …?

A **Choose one of the events below that you remember, or go online and choose a different historic event that has occurred in your lifetime.**

- June 22, 1986 – Diego Maradona's "Hand of God" goal
- November 10, 1989 – the fall of the Berlin wall
- April 5, 1994 – the death of Kurt Cobain
- December 31, 2000 – the world prepared for Y2K … and nothing happened
- December 5, 2013 – the death of Nelson Mandela

B **Make notes about what you remember most about the event you chose.**

C **In your next class, describe the event and what you remember about it. Do your classmates remember the event as well? Do their memories match yours?**

NOTES

The authors and publishers acknowledge the following sources of copyright material and are grateful for the permissions granted. While every effort has been made, it has not always been possible to identify the sources of all the material used, or to trace all copyright holders. If any omissions are brought to our notice, we will be happy to include the appropriate acknowledgments on reprinting and in the next update to the digital edition, as applicable.

Photographs
Key: B = Below, BL = Below Left, BR = Below Right, C = Centre, CL = Centre Left, CR = Centre Right, TC = Top Centre, TL = Top Left, TR = Top Right.

All the photographs are sourced from Getty Images.

p. 50: Zero Creatives/Cultura; p. 52: PeopleImages/E+; p. 54: Phil Boorman/Cultura; p. 56: photosoup/iStock/Getty Images Plus; p. 59: Tara Moore/Taxi; p. 60: Image Source/Seb Oliver; p. 61: Igor Ustynskyy/Moment; p. 62: ImagesBazaar; p. 63: yanyong/iStock/Getty Images Plus; p. 64: levente bodo/Moment; p. 66 (TL): Joe_Potato/iStock/Getty Images Plus; p. 66 (TR): WIN-Initiative; p. 66 (TC): Alan Schein Photography/Corbis; p. 66 (CL): Comstock/Stockbyte; p. 66 (TR): Andrey Rudakov/Bloomberg; p. 66 (C): Teddy Morduhovich/EyeEm; p. 66 (BL): Wayne Eastep/Photographer's Choice; p. 66 (BC): YOSHIHIRO TAKADA/a.collectionRF; p. 66 (BR): Caiaimage/Sam Edwards; p. 67: Creatas/Getty Images Plus; p. 68: Photograph by Bernd Zillich/Moment; p. 69: Mike Powell/Allsport Concepts; p. 70: stsvirkun/iStock/Getty Images Plus; p. 71 (TR): Tom Merton/Caiaimage; p. 71 (B), p. 83: Ariel Skelley/DigitalVision; p. 72: Bettmann; p. 74: undefined undefined/iStock/Getty Images Plus; p. 75, p. 95: Westend61; p. 76: bowdenimages/iStock/Getty Images Plus; p. 77: Mario Castello/Corbis; p. 78: aapskyiStock/Getty Images Plus; p. 79: Bobex-73/iStock/Getty Images Plus; p. 80: SergioProvilskyi/iStock/Getty Images Plus; p. 82: Fuse/Corbis; p. 85: Juzant/DigitalVision; p. 86: Portra Images/DigitalVision; p. 87: pawel.gaul/E+; p. 88: Hulton Archive; p. 91: typhoonski/iStock/Getty Images Plus; p. 92: Roetting+Pollex/LOOK; p. 94: Denis Torkhov/iStock/Getty Images Plus; p. 96: Kane Skennar/DigitalVision.

Front cover photography by Alija/E+.

Audio production by CityVox, New York.

Corpus
Development of this publication has made use of the Cambridge English Corpus (CEC). The CEC is a multi-billion word collection of contemporary spoken and written English. It includes British English, American English, and other varieties. It also includes the Cambridge Learner Corpus, the world's biggest collection of learner writing, developed in collaboration with Cambridge Assessment. Cambridge University Press uses the CEC to provide evidence about language use that helps to produce better language teaching materials. Our Evolve authors study the Corpus to see how English is really used, and to identify typical learner mistakes. This information informs the authors' selection of vocabulary, grammar items and Student's Book Corpus features such as the Accuracy Check, Register Check, and Insider English.